Spinning Upward

Spinning Upward

Feminine Solutions

Patsy Seo

To order additional copies of this book, contact:
Xlibris Corporation
1-888-795-4274
www.Xlibris.com
Orders@Xlibris.com
84281

Contents

The Drive-by

AMBER STARED OUT the window at the rain, which was washing away, the blood pouring from under her lovers still corpse. Her lover's blood ran across the hard sidewalk and down the curb into the sewer. She felt like her heart had been ripped out of her chest. Her lover, that talented happy youth from the other side of town; only minutes ago, he had made her heart sing, as he serenaded her window. Her lover had blond hair and his blue eyes shown with his love for her. Only a few minutes earlier The day was full of bright sun and a bright future. Then came the ancient black Cadillac, driving swiftly around the corner. The flash of fire from the Saturday night special. Now he lay dead from another drive by shooting. It seemed instantly, there was a flash of lightning from the heavens, and a torrent of rain poured down to wash away his blood

Gang Lords controlled her Neighborhood. Drugs were the biggest commercial enterprise south of the railroad tracks. Strangers from the other side of the tracks were not welcome. She cried silently, and stared quietly. Something in her died. She thought she would never live again. Her mother washed dishes, quiet, efficient, her heart cold, empty cold sad thoughts passed through her mind, as she tried to logically sort through the unthinkable. She didn't care for the young white lover of her daughter. The very first time she saw him; she knew at once, that he was trouble. She just knew her daughters' heart would be broken.

She had tried to keep them apart. He was a good boy, from the other side of town. His parents wanted no part of her black daughter, from the lower side.

She wanted no part of them. She and they agreed on this, at least. She had no doubt their love had been genuine, but that only meant more pain for her daughter. Amber, herself, had warned her lover not to be caught in her neighborhood. She, at least partially understood, the risk he was taking. Amber had told her mother, how patiently, she had tried to explain all this to him, but their worlds were so different; he could not understand the dangers of her world. Now as the mother quietly, and carefully, put another dish in the cupboard; she startled herself, "Oh my God! I have got to call his parents" It hadn't occurred to her, to call anyone. People in her neighborhood, just didn't call the police; but now the circumstances were changed. This young man, from a white neighborhood was visiting her daughter; and now he was lying on the sidewalk, doubtless dead; and no one from the other world, on the other side of the tracks would understand.

They would blame someone. Oh my God! She had been so quiet, living alone and trying to raise this daughter, her most precious possession, by being quiet like the mouse behind the cupboard. Now like the mouse she was trapped, and the spotlight would turn to her and somehow; she and her daughter would be blamed, for luring the innocent to his death. The mother picked up the phone and dialed. "Mrs. Williams, this is Marcie, Amber's mother. Are you sitting down?

Mrs. Williams had been standing by the sink, as she lifted the wall phones receiver from its cradle. Now, she grabbed a kitchen chair, and sat down with a thud at the table. She knew Amber's mother, Marcie Jackson, well enough to know she hadn't called for a friendly chitchat.

Her throat closed with fear; but she managed to get out, in an almost natural voice, "Marcie, how nice of you to call" "I was just" But Marcie interrupted her,

"Mrs. Williams, I don't know how to tell you this" and she paused. Now Mrs. Janet Williams was really frightened, If there was something that Marcie the Emergency room nurse didn't know how to say . . . . Janet really couldn't speak this time. All she could do, was sit in dumb struck silence, and wait with dread for words for words . . . her thoughts just stopped coming, and her mind went blank as the freshly washed dish Mrs. Jackson had been holding moments before; fell from her hand and broke on the floor. Marcie just said it straight out "Something terrible has happened, your son has been shot, right in front of my apartment. Mrs. Jackson was now automatically speaking She felt numb and unable to think at all. She listened to her own words as she replied, "How did it happen? How badly is he hurt? It was as if she were drowning and grasping for a straw. Then she suddenly said, I will be right over.

Mrs. Williams replied "Yes, I think that would be a good idea and perhaps you might want to call your husband and ask him to leave work early and come with you"

"No, No wait. Don't come here, meet us at the Emergency Room of Middletown General Hospital." Amber's mother put the receiver carefully back down, on the old dial phone, on the table, then called 911. She had lost her mouse like fear, and was back in work mode, Nurse style.

Grabbing her shoulder length purse, She turned to Amber and said; "Amber, come with me, I need your help." Amber's personality instantly changed as well. She recognized Nurse Jackson, came to attention, grabbed her sweater and an umbrella, and meekly followed her out of the house. When they arrived curbside, Amber's mother found to her delight and surprise, that she had been mistaken. Bobby was not yet dead, just knocked out cold. Life returned to his cold blue face. He opened his eyes, gasped for air, and smiled gently up at Amber. "Lie still!" Commanded Nurse Jackson She quickly assessed the damage.

The bullet had hit a rib and was stuck, still visible, where the rib met the breastbone. The bullet had hit with enough force, to knock the air out of him. When he fell backwards: his head hit the curb. Could his neck be broken? She didn't think so: but just in case she turned back to her daughter and said, "Fetch the ironing board" It was then; she saw that a crowd of neighbors had gathered around her. Her daughter ran off immediately, and Nurse Jackson asked, "Does anyone have one of those bunji ropes to tie down cargo in a truck. Tawin Lee spoke up first, "No but I can lend you a pair of my suspenders." Mrs. Jackson replied quickly, "That will do nicely"

She wanted to put pressure to the wound on Bobby's chest but the rib was probably broken and could puncture his lung. She pulled out two packages of Kleenex from her purse unwrapped them and made a pad for pressure on his head wound. The most of the blood had come from there. She secured it with long strips of micropore paper tape.

Amber reappeared carrying the ironing board and her new gold elastic belt. With the red suspenders supplied by Mr. Lee and her daughter's shinny gold belt, Nurse Jackson carefully secured Bobby to the ironing board, just as the ambulance arrived.

Mrs. Jackson greeted the Ambulance driver, and the EMT, as they drove up.

"I immobilized him for you, just slide the board onto the gurney"

She didn't bother to mention The board was her ironing board. "Yes, ma'am", they replied in unison. Jack the driver and Charles the EMT, were accustomed to taking orders from Mrs. Jackson, Surgery's charge nurse. "It is almost time for me to report to work so, we will follow you in our car", Mrs. Jackson continued.

Amber was holding tightly to her lover's hand. "No mother. I want to ride in the ambulance with Bobby" Mrs. Jackson replied, "very well'. Jack and Charles exchanged a glance, but neither spoke. Charles was holding up the IV bag as Mrs. Jackson inserted the IV needle. They quickly loaded Bobby's gurney into the ambulance. Amber was on Charles's side of the gurney. Charles managed to get Amber seated on the Ambulance bench next to her lover, without disengaging her hand from Bobbies. He climbed in as he hung the IV bag on its hanger and sat on the bench on the other side of the gurney.

Mrs. Jackson shut the Ambulance doors as she yelled to Jack, "Your passengers are secure. You are ready to go." Jack, with sirens blaring, roared off toward Middletown Hospital.

Mrs. Jackson, in her beat up old Mustang got there first. She was waiting to open the Ambulance doors as soon as it stopped. On the short trip to the hospital Amber bent over Bobby, tears running down her cheek, she lay her head, gently next to his wounded chest. Bobby for his part was content to lay quietly, still attached with his bright suspenders to Mrs. Jackson's ironing board Amber's being there, holding his hand, eased the pain that was mounting in his chest. It was almost time for Marcie's shift to begin so she went on into the Emergency Room with Bobby and donned a pair of scrubs, Mrs. Jackson separated Bobbie and Amber with, "Amber you will have to wait with Mr. and Mrs. Williams in the waiting room for news of Bobby. Amber, looking around the ER waiting room, saw her best friend, Beth, sitting next to a vacant seat with her mother Janice from Dr David's office. Beth and Amber were in Dr Ludlow's class and regular opponents in the ethics discussions that took place under Dr Ludlow's supervision after school. Mr. and Mrs. Williams in their new gold Porsche pulled into the Middletown Hospital Parking Lot, fifteen minutes behind the ambulance that carried Bobby

They ran frantically into the ER waiting room. Looking around for Bobby, they saw Amber There were no free seats on her side of the waiting room. Mrs. Williams sat down next to Mrs. Ludlow, who was waiting to be seen. Mrs. Ludlow, despite suffering headache and nausea from her cancer chemotherapy, looked up at Mrs. Williams with a welcoming smile. Mrs. Williams had welcomed the Ludlow's with a plate of cookies and offers to help, when the Ludlow's moved in next door to them. Since then the two families had been good friends. Mr. Ludlow gestured for Mr. Williams to sit down beside him as he inquired, "Wasn't that Bobby I saw being wheeled into the ER a few minutes ago." "What happened?" "He looked like he had a chest wound" "He did," Mr. Williams replied." Drive by shooting.""Oh no!" Ludlow said looking concerned, "Was he visiting that Jackson girl, He is so sweet on"

"Ah yes, How did you know?" came out slowly from Mr. Williams, as he seated himself next to Mr. Ludlow and gaped open mouthed in surprise.

Mr. Ludlow talked at length about Amber and Beth, and his after school ethics class, as Mrs. Williams and

Mrs. Ludlow, sat quietly holding hands, listening, and giving silent comfort to each other. Mrs. Ludlow felt her headache and nausea disappear. Mrs. William relaxed and lost some of her fear for Bobby, as she thought about how brave, Mr. and Mrs. Ludlow were, in the face of her terminal cancer. Mr. Ludlow invited Mr. and Mrs. Williams to attend his after school ethics class. Mr. Williams said he would try and Mrs. Williams said she would look forward to it with pleasure. Bobby had been sent on to X-Ray with Marcie at his side. The ER nurse motioned for Mrs. Ludlow to come in. Just as Mr. Ludlow got up from his seat to take Mrs. Ludlow into the examining room. Mr. Lattimer came thru the door escorting his mother Mrs. Pike.

"Bill, Let me introduce you and your mother to Mr. and Mrs. Williams, they are waiting for their son who has been shot." Mrs. Pike was excited to hear everything. Bill replied, "What happened" just as Mr. Ludlow had done earlier. Mr. Williams relayed the whole event, this time with less self pity and more self confidence. He ended up his monologue with "what brings you and your mother to the emergency room?""We think mom sprained her wrist hanging onto her cane, you see, Beth sped by Mrs. Pike, riding her new racer, and nearly knocked her down. Mom heard her coming and braced herself, grasping the fancy Ram's horn handle on her cane with both hands, or she would have bowled her over." He continued on with the entire story, entertaining Mrs. Williams, so she almost completely forgot to worry about her son, Bobby. Mrs. Pike hobbled along, barely making snail like progress with her cane, toward the House where she lived with her son and his family. Her son Bill Lattimer, who had been watching from the upstairs window, stuck his head out and yelled, "Beth, if I ever see you and that bike on my lawn again, I will throw you both up on the roof" "Yeh right" was Mr. Williams's comment. Bill immediately replied, "Believe it or not, there was a time when I could have." That was a long time ago, I sometimes forget I am not the young stud I was once" and then continued on relating the whole story to Mr. Williams Bill was athletic and well built, for his age. He was the High School mathematics teacher. He had been a race car driver while he was studying for his college degree and teaching certificate. No one messed with him in those days.

No one really knew his real age. It was known that he taught at the High School when it first opened, more than 60 years ago. As for his mother, she had been living in that same house for longer than anyone remember. He met Mrs. Pike at the front door wishing he had left his bills and computer sooner, and escorted her to the house as soon as she drove up. Now he turned his full attention his full attention to Mrs. Pike. "Mom are you all right?" "Yes

Bill, I am fine, Just a little shook up" Mr. Lattimer could see she was not fine. She could barely stand for the violent shaking, and her wrist had started to swell up like a balloon and change colors. He respected his mother; She was 105 She still drove the car and liked to be independent, but this wasn't the first time the neighborhood children had nearly knocked her down. She had suffered a broken wrist from grabbing the cane handle so tightly so Bill Lattimer saved his work, shut down his computer and drove his Mom to the Middletown General Hospital Emergency Room instead of finishing up his bills as he had planned.

Sitting in the waiting room Bill Lattimer reflected on the pros and cons of having his mother live with them. She was growing older and he and his wife had discussed what would happen as she got older and required more care. It had worried them a lot when they first decided to live with his mother. That was just after his father died, more than 50 years ago

After the funeral his mother had discussed selling the house and getting a smaller place just for herself but they needed a home and were expecting their first child. She offered to have them move in with her. It was Mrs. Pike's house. She and her husband had lived there, together, for forty years. During that time they had raised six sons. They always wanted a girl but after the sixth son they decided it was time, to just accept their fate, and enjoy their boys. Mrs. Pike worked for Woolworths long past time for her to retire. They went out of business and she never tried to find a job anyplace else She had talked of retiring when her husband Roger had retired from Black's Shoe Factory. Mr. Pike hadn't really wanted to retire but because of Union rules he had to when he became 65.

He had a number of large machines in their basement. He could make all sorts of custom parts, precise to within a thousandth of a millimeter. His father had affectionately called the basement his doll house Certainly, not many people had a doll house to retire to; but then not many people had raised six mechanically inclined sons. Bill was the youngest, and the only one that didn't work with machines. He had always lived at home and went on to get a college degree in Mathematics and Music. Everything had gone well for them so far. His mom's health had held up and he had been very lucky. They had the girl, his mom and dad had always wanted. She was a darling. He smiled as he remembered seeing his little girl for the first time

Then finishing up his long story with. "She was nothing like Beth. She was always polite and studious" "That was a long time ago, Mrs. Lattimer stayed home and made sure her little girl was properly behaved and motivated. She grew up long ago and now has a law practice and a family of her own.

Marcie came over to Mr. and Mrs. Williams and told them that Bobby was going to be all right. "I went with him to surgery and assisted while they operated to remove the bullet from his rib." Dr. Gordon said he had never seen one lodge in a rib that way, it is really unusual because the ribs are hard." "He said Bobby's ribs look normal, and maybe it was just because the bullet had an unusually sharp tip." "Dr. Gordon made an appointment for Bobby to see the bone specialist in four months. He also sent copies of Bobby's X-Rays to him."

Mr. Lattimer saw Mrs. Pike coming back out of the Emergency room. He stood up preparing to leave as he said to his mother, "What did Dr. Gordon say?". Mrs. Pike grinned as she replied "He said it was broken, and I should be more careful, as I would take longer to heal than most people. He said I am not as young as I used to be. You think?", and she grinned again. Mrs. Ludlow and Mr. Williams were right behind him and Mr. Ludlow repeated to his wife, "What Mr. Lattimer had just asked his mother. "What did Dr. Gordon say?" She replied "He gave me another prescription for nausea and headache and made an appointment with my oncologist, for day after tomorrow." As Mr. Lattimer held open the door for his mother and Mrs. Ludlow to leave, he glanced around the waiting room. He saw that Marcie was still talking to Mr. and Mrs. Williams and wondered how Bobby was doing. Amber was standing behind her mother, holding Beth's hand and listening intently.

He would find out later in class from the two girls how Bobby was and if he would be able to return to school this year. Just then Arnold and his buddy came barreling thru the ER door. "Like Father like daughter Mr. Lattimer said over his shoulder to Mr. Ludlow with raised eyebrows, and faked outrage."

"Looks, like they missed Bobby at the shooting scene." was Mr. Ludlow's reply. "They have egg all over their face now. They took their sweet time to respond to Marcie's call from the wrong side of town, where she lives, only to discover the victim was an honors student from one of the town's prominent citizens." "Obviously, they don't know Marcie very well."

Marcie takes back her neighborhood

MR. LUDLOW WAS half right. Arnold and his buddy had responded quickly. They were surprised, that the victim was Bobby. They were there to see him being driven off to the hospital. The reason, that they were delayed was even more surprising than the shooting. Marcie had all her neighbors lined up to talk them and be witness to the shooting that occurred. Arnold couldn't believe his eyes. No one in that neighborhood ever saw anything. Now they were clamoring to testify all about the shooting of an outsider, no less. Arnold and his buddy started interviewing them one by one and writing it all down on their clip boards. By the time they had written everything down and made several trips with the neighbors to the station more than an hour had passed. Arnold and his buddy were not ones to pass up a "golden opportunity" and they had just struck gold big-time. They wanted to be sure they had mug shots identified and sketches drawn of the shooters plus any other relevant clues Marcie's neighbors were willing to share. Marcie and her daughter were involved. That was the only difference between this drive by shooting and any other. The neighbors all knew and loved Amber. Marcie had gradually become their first and sometimes only medical resource. Amber had grown up in the neighborhood. She was precocious and friendly with everyone. In Kindergarten, Amber's teacher, Miss Spirit had called Marcie to tell her that Amber needed to learn to how tie her shoes. Marcie was very surprised. She knew Amber had been dressing herself, and tie-ing her shoes for a long time. She thought there must be a mistake and asked Miss Spirit, "are you sure you don't have Amber mixed up with another student." "I am sure." Miss Spirit replied and described Amber and what she was wearing to school that day. As soon as Marcie saw Amber she asked, "Amber, What is going on with you at school? Miss Spirit says you can't tie your shoes? I know you can." Amber looked at Marcie, with a serous expression on her face. "I don't want my teacher to know I can tie my shoes. I want Elroy to tie them for me." Marcie just smiled at

Amber, as she said firmly, "I am sorry Amber, but you have to tie your own shoes in Miss Spirit's class Elroy was Amber's favorite trash heap playmate. One day Amber had come running into their apartment. As she ran up to her mother she said, "Mommy, it is time for you! Elroy cut off his toes." Marcie had been working in the kitchen. Her heart nearly jumped out of her chest as. She dropped everything to run out with Amber. Elroy was bleeding profusely from his bare toes. She picked up the frightened Elroy and carried him into her kitchen. She instructed Amber to fetch a clean towel and the betadine, as she inspected Elroy's bleeding foot.

He had stepped on a broken bottle and it was true that he had a nasty cut but Marcie silently thanked God to see his toes were still firmly attached. She stopped the bleeding, bandaged his foot and carried Elroy to his home. She had no idea where Elroy lived; but Elroy pointed the way. She was glad to see that Elroy's mother was home. She handed Elroy over to his mother explaining what had happened, what she had done about it and telling his mother to take Elroy to see their doctor. Elroy's mother was very grateful but they had no money, no insurance and no Doctor. Elroy's foot healed up just fine. His mother did make sure, he got new shoes, and wore them all the time till the foot healed up completely. Marcie never had time to meet new people and socialize but she always opened her door to neighbors with a medical emergency and starting with the children, then their mothers it became known that she could be counted on.

When unemployment climbed to double digits many of her neighbors could not even afford food. Street drugs had been available only a few blocks from her house. Marcie was aware that gangs controlled her neighborhood. She tried to live quietly, sharing peanut butter sandwiches with the children, who were Amber's friends. Amber was an honors student and stayed out of trouble. When she had time she baked her favorite recipe for red velvet chocolate cake with fudge icing, or made maple syrup toffee, chock full of nuts. She used whatever nuts she had, and called the recipe she invented herself, after studying polymers in chemistry, "Everyone's favorite nut toffee" Marcie never complained, never asked for help, but was always ready to lend a helping hand. Most women, who made her salary would have moved to the other side of town long ago. Marcie attended the small Baptist Church a few blocks away. She liked the Pastor and the church's interest in the children of the community. She felt more welcome, and safer, in the black community, than next to more affluent white folks. She saved every penny she could for her and Amber's future. Now, when she needed it, first Tawin Lee, who was the night shift clerk for Jay's cheap run down hotel, offered his help. Then the other neighbors quickly fell in line. Nearly, all of them had received her help, at one time or another. She would always reply, if someone asked how they could repay her kindness. "No thanks are needed for good deeds, Just pass it on." Arnold and his buddy had no knowledge of Marcie's relationship with the community but after taking notes from her neighbors and driving some of them to the Police station, Arnold and his buddy went to Middletown Hospital to talk to Marcie and Amber. Their timing was perfect. Marcie was talking to Mr. and Mrs. Williams and was ready for her first break. After passing the Ludlow and Lattimer couple, They ran up to the ER receptionist who was happy to point out Marcie in the waiting room to them. Marcie suggested they all go to the hospital cafeteria that was just opening, and have an early lunch. Arnold and his buddy were hungry. They were already thinking they would be able get a murder conviction on the drive by shooters. This was the first big break they had had on gangs in Marcie's community.

Arnold, seeing that Mr. and Mrs. Williams, seemed remarkably calm turned first to Mr. Williams, and asked, "What did Dr. Gordon say about Bobby?" Arnold and his buddy tried not to look to disappointed as Mr. Williams related all that Dr. Gordon had said, and included as an afterthought, that they would be able to question him themselves, when he got out of the recovery room.

Marcie's 15 minute break stretched well beyond two hours, as they discussed the shooting and continued on to plans to take back the neighborhood from the drug dealers. Arnold and Marcie were both exuberant at her neighbor's turnout. She let it slip that she was acquainted with members of the largest motorcycle gang in the area. They were all ex cons. She knew that in order to pay off the income tax that the government found out they owed on drug profits when they were arrested, they often had to continue to sell drugs. She felt the gang members, like her and her neighbors, wanted to live in peace and survive. Arnold and his buddy were straight shooting cops. They had no intention of becoming crooked cops.

It was all news to Mr. and Mrs. Williams. Mrs. Williams was all questions and frequently uttered the phrase "but it is not safe for decent people" "my son was shot' Several times she was on the verge of breaking down in tears.

Marcie got called on her pager and ended the conversation with "I just have to go." Arnold and Mr. Williams started fighting over the check when Mr. Williams said, "How about I let you pick up the check this time and tonight we all meet at my house for dinner at 6." Looking at Marcie he said, "You in?" Marcie replied embarrassed, "I am not familiar with that side of town, I have no idea where you live." Arnold immediately spoke up, "I know where it is." "I will pick you and Amber up in Bobby's room, just before visiting hours are over and drive you there in the squad car." After dinner, I can drive you and Amber back to your apartment. Mrs. Williams spoke up this time, "It's settled then"

What everyone needs is a good mother-in-law

MARY DARLENE WAITE had climbed half way up Green Mountain. She joined the Green Mountaineers once a week to hike half way up She was an attractive and successful black business woman.

She was glad to see Jane the town gossip sitting half way up the hill, waiting to spill the latest gossip Mary Darlene remembered that last week: Jane had surprised her with all sorts of questions about her personal life. Taken by surprise she replied that she was fat, forty and very out of shape. The main reason she enjoyed the weekly outings with the Green Mountaineers was the dinner after and watching Arnold's muscles glisten in the sun. Jane looked shocked at her honest reply. She had expected something a bit more vague and professional. Once the words were out there was no taking them back and after a few minutes staring with open mouth Jane accepted her matter of fact statement and agreed.

The rest of the morning they sat in silence. Now she was recalling the events of her life, that had brought her to this place in her life. She would have preferred to leave the past, in the past; but she considered answering Jane's questions, as the price she had to pay to hear the latest town gossip. She thought, "not everyone hates a gossip. Most people enjoy listening just not about themselves." Everyone seems to care who their birth parents are.

I however, don't see what it's really about.

I never knew my real parents. The Waites weren't my real parents. My real parents were the hired hands, the Freedmans. I have six brothers and sisters named Freedman and four named Waite I was born on a plantation in Lincoln, Georgia to "former "slaves. My Great Great Granddaddy fought for the South and never left the service of the Master. My mother christened me Mary Darlene just before she died. My mother had a black midwife, and died of complications of childbirth, a few hours after I was born. My daddy was devastated, when my mother died. He couldn't really care for a newborn He already had six children to care for; and I would have made seven. The older children could take care of the three year old. A newborn was something else. Mrs. Waite, the plantation owner's wife, took me as her own. My birth mother had produced six healthy children in only five years. The doctor at the free health clinic had told her not to have anymore. She didn't, until she thought she was through the change of life and I took her by surprise Mrs. Waite the plantation owner's wife already had 4 other children. All of them, were out of the house, and in school. She accepted me as a present from God, and became my Foster mother. I was taught reverence for God, and the appreciation of hand me downs. Gerald Waite her oldest son was the archetypical spoiled brat. He had a gorgeous build, blond curly hair, and he sat his Arabian Stallion like a God. Growing up with him, I had to endure his taunts and give up anything of mine he took a fancy to. It really shouldn't have been a surprise to anyone when I was raped by Mrs. Waite's oldest son, Gerald.

Gerald was thirty, and I was sixteen. His "Love" for me was not welcomed by me or his parents. I just hated his guts. It didn't help that I knew he slept around town, and occasionally beat up some hapless woman that crossed him. His parents didn't think I was good enough for him. They didn't want their blond Adonis marrying a black woman. I contracted syphilis from him, which left me infertile for life. I would like to leave the past in the past. Some of it is not something I want to remember, but "it is what it is" My foster mother loved me in her own way; but I had become an embarrassment to her, and myself. Her strong family pride, misplaced on her son, was a part of her, I accepted. At eighteen, I graduated from Lincoln High School. Two months later I moved north to Greenridge, California. I had aced accounting and math in High School. I accepted a job in a new branch of Bank of America which had just been opened up in Greenridge, California I found the job advertised in brochures in the Lincoln High School Counselor's office. I took business and accounting courses while working full time at the Bank.

Mary Darlene's Earned Success

I HAVE BEEN working for the Bank of America here, ever since. The last year of High School I worked summers for the Dairy Freeze and the evening shift bagging Groceries for Lincoln's Alpha Beta Grocery store. I saved up money for the train fare, a business suit and enough to get me settled comfortably in my own apartment. I went to Mexico with the Jackson Family. They owned the Greenridge Sizzler's Franchise. I had agreed to straighten out their bookkeeping, they would take me on vacation to Guadalajara, Mexico. While on vacation with them in Guadalajara, I met and fell in love with Jose Gutierrez. I got up early and worked on the books while the rest of the Jackson family slept in. I was accepted by them and the locals as "their daughter" while I was there. I suppose being the only black daughter of an all white family should have seemed odd to me, but then how could it? Jose Gutierrez was working as cook, chauffeur, and all around handy man. He also house sat for them when they were back working in Greenridge. He also felt like a semi adopted member of the Jackson family. Jose was a tall good looking Latin who shared my interest in accounting. He asked me help him set up his own set of "books: to keep track of household expenses. In return he brought me coffee and eggs for breakfast, before I started on the Sizzler accounting books. Mary Darlene found true Love.

We soon became an item. I went with him, when he drove the Jacksons around time. We were quite the handsome couple. I fell desperately in love. He loved me as well. At first, I thought we were the perfect couple. With the Jackson family around, we seemed the perfect fit. We both wanted to have a family. I was not only, incapable of having children, because the syphilis had made me sterile; I soon found out that I was a shameless black American woman, in his mothers' eyes. In the end, Jose married his mother's choice. It seemed, at first he had made a good choice. His mother was very happy as Maria was at first a dutiful wife, and had two baby boys.

Jose's mother couldn't have been more proud. Maria got bored with being a housewife and mother. She left him to run off to America with an American Soldier on leave. His father died a few years later. José's' mother moved in to help take care of his two sons. Their mother just left them behind for her soldier boy.

So that is how it is now. Eighteen years after meeting Jose, the Love of my life: I am the single female manager of the local Bank of America. Jose now owns the house and Restaurant he used to manage for the Jackson's. He also owns a local Restaurant and Bar. He like myself, is now also successful but alone and lonely. Jose and I are again talking of "our love" again. His boys joined his ex-wife in America last year after Grandma died. Her soldier boy turned out to be a devoted husband and father. She had two more boys by him, before she mentioned, she missed the two she left behind. It wasn't hard for her to reconnect with Jose and his family, as they were right where she left them. I wrote a letter to Jose, and mailed it at the Post Office on my way, to the Green Mountain Club hike. Mary Darlene stopped to rest one third of the way up Green Mountain, sitting down next to Jane She was prepared this time but Jane didn't ask any more embarrassing questions. She waited there for the rest of the Green Mountaineers, especially Arnold to come back down the Mountain. Green Mountain is really only a small hill in the middle of town, but the closest thing to a mountain in the city of Greenridge. After the strenuous hike, we will eat at the Green Mountain Inn. The Inn and Arnold are the real reason I'm part of the club. I just abhorred exercise; but the idea of seeing Arnold could get me to the Green Mountain Club meetings on Sunday afternoons. I knew he was happily married and I certainly had no plans to complicate my life with romancing a honky police officer Arnold Whitaker is a handsome Police man. He is brave, perhaps too brave, handsome and at the prime of his life. His daughter Beth, was 16 or 17 slightly overweight, average looking nice young lady. I knew and liked his wife Janice. She worked long hours for Mercy Clinic. She was Head Nurse, Administrator, Girl Friday, Secretary and sometime Security Guard or Handy Man.

Dr David was well over ninety and would have retired years ago but no one could be found to take his place. Dr David and Janice kept the clinic going, just because it was needed and they were "Good People". I chided myself mentally, as I waited and looked forward to seeing Arnold come back over the top of the mountain, his bulging muscles glistening in the sun. He was Picking his way carefully ahead of the others and cautioning the tender foots to look out for loose rocks and other hazards.

I was closer to Dr David in age, than to Arnold, and should have been contemplating him. He was a distinguished looking single man with flawless white hair and manners. I never saw him without a shirt and tie. Let's face it. I was old but not dead! I thought to myself, "Muscles always did get my attention." Arnold really turned my head and I enjoyed being with him. He was always the first to make the hike up Green Mountain. I usually only made it part way. Jane came back down first. She had gone up another third of the way and turned around and came back down to rest with me Jane had been Janice and Arnold's next door neighbor for 20 years. She was quite a gossip. I was glad to see her and waved hello. This time I was prepared with better answers for her question, but instead, She sat down next to me as she said "it is a shame about Janice Whitaker". "Why, what do you mean? Janice is Arnold's wife isn't she?" "Yes, but don't you know she filed for divorce from Arnold", Jane replied? "No I didn't know, and frankly I am shocked." "Why, on ever for"?, Was my reply. "Arnold looks like the perfect catch to me and Janice was always a sensible young woman." Jane proceeded to tell me the story of the mess they were in. Beth was their only child and Janice had given her everything she wanted. She always had the nicest dresses, best electronic gadgets and Christmas always brought her heart's desire. Beth reciprocated, by being a problem, from the time she left home, by herself, at only two years old. She was following a little stray kitten into a very rough neighborhood. Janice and Arnold spent hours searching for her. Arnold had several of his buddies on the force join in. Finally Krueger the town drunk approached one of the buddies with the little girl and the kitten in tow. Officer Bill Andrews knew Krueger. He knew Krueger was known for being a mean drunk. Krueger usually never approached the police: in fact, He hid from them. Officer Andrews was at first surprised, but would soon find out why this was a big exception. Beth wanted his cat. Officer Andrews could easily understand that Beth was a big problem; Krueger could not deal with in his condition.

Krueger was known for being a mean drunk, but Beth wanted his cat. The kitten was a stray, Krueger had rescued from Putters pond. Someone wrapped it, and two other kittens in a bag weighed down with a brick, and tossed them in the pond to drown. The two others were dead, but Krueger rescued the third, and took it back to his card board box.

He shared the last of his supper except for the whiskey, and they both went to sleep. Kittens are nocturnal. The little kitten woke up early in the morning, hungry. No one responded to its mewing. The man had drunk almost a whole fifth, and was passed out cold. The kitten would have left sooner looking for a hand out, but the man was warm and the night was cold. Finally, the sun came up, and the kitten finding it warmer went out to search for food. Beth saw it knock over a bottle of milk on Jane's porch and lap hungrily till it was satisfied. She started toward it. The kitten took off for the only safety it knew, the town drunk. I guess, even comatose, being mauled by a giggling toddler playing with a timid kitten trying to hide in whatever warm crevasse it could find, finally woke up the town drunk. Krueger sat there groggy, with his a nasty hangover trying to think what he should do. He avoided children as they were big trouble. His reputation, as a mean drunk was a carefully executed sham to keep away children, who either taunted him, or were followed by irate parents, wanting to protect them, from the dirty old man. Krueger couldn't think because his head hurt, he was still groggy from sleep, and the whiskey. This development took him totally by surprise. So when the little girl stopped, and looked up for a second, when she heard Bill Andrews fellow officer yelling "Beth"; Krueger took the little girls hand and as he held the kitten securely under his jacket where it had taken refuge, and was digging in its claws. He started off toward the voice, asking the little girl in a voice husky and gruff with whiskey. "Isn't your name Beth?" Beth looked up at this big man with the gruff voice and replied meekly, "yes" That was enough for Krueger. Krueger usually hid from the police, unless it was really cold out. He didn't want to spend the night in the local jail too often, for "drunk and disorderly. "He was saving that offense, for times when he might freeze to death, if not for a warm bed. Bill usually avoided the harmless old drunk as well. He did not want to waste his time. With him and He had a soft spot for old Krueger. He knew he had once been a hard working man before he fell on hard times. He also knew the mean drunk act was put on for self protection. This time they hurried toward each other like long lost friends. Bill was looking to find what Krueger was anxious to part with. Krueger hadn't meant to give up the kitten. It was after all, his one only friend; but Beth wasn't going to part with it easily; Krueger was anxious to get her off his back, and out of his jacket. Cute and cuddly as she was, she looked like more trouble than he could handle. Krueger gave Officer Bill Andrews Beth's' hand and handed him the kitten. Krueger started to back away when Officer Bill Andrews said, "Hold on there just a minute. I want you to sit in the back seat of the squad car with Beth and the kitten. I don't want Beth or the kitten loose in the car while I try to drive her back home." Krueger started to object; but it was easy to see that Officer Bill would have none of it; as he continued with, "Maybe Janice will give you a bottle of aspirin, and a bath as a finder's fee." So he just mumbled weakly, "OK" as he climbed in the back seat, and secured the kitten again, inside his dirty jacket. Beth, eyes wide, climbed happily up on the seat beside him, and continually giggling, pursued and petted the frightened little kitten. Krueger scared half out of his wits sat quietly and endured it all without complaint. Officer Andrews drove off thinking. "Jessie, his pet name for the squad car, I promise I will take you straight to the car wash, as soon as I drop off these three, at Janice's house. Krueger hadn't had a bath recently. Man he stunk! He probably hadn't bathed since the pond got cold early September, and this was almost time for the spring thaw."

"Jessie is going to need to be aired out and deodorized. "Maybe, I will stop by the grocery and pickup a can of room spray, and a sandwich for my lunch on the way to the car wash" When Officer Andrews dropped off the three of them at Janice's' house. She was so happy to see Beth safe and sound she made no comment about the kitten, or Officer Andrews' promise she would reward Krueger with a bottle of aspirin and a warm bath. She just looked at Krueger with that welcoming smile of hers, thinking to herself, "You DO need a bath" "Mr. Krueger if you will just follow me this way I think I can find one of Arnold's extra suits." At this, Arnold who had been standing with his mouth open, listening to Officer Bill's explanations, and not knowing what to think, turned in the direction of Krueger and Janice saying, "Oh yes, I have an extra suit. I'll go with you Krueger while Janice takes care of Beth and the kitten." Arnold had reasoned: given the choice of defleaing/delousing the kitten, as well as washing and changing an excited Beth into clean clothes: Not to mention, getting her to settle down for her Nap; Finding a clean towel and old suit of his, for Krueger would be an easy job.

Upstairs in the family bathroom, Arnold looked at Krueger sternly as he handed him one of his clean but worn out old suits and a fresh towel. "Krueger "he said "I am glad you and Officer Andrews found Beth, but I don't know, what he was thinking, dropping you and that kitten off with Janice like that." Krueger's thoughts were interrupted by Arnold's words. Krueger had just been thinking, "I haven't felt this good in a long time. I am not the least bit groggy and even my headache is completely gone!"

"Maybe it was the scare Officer Bill gave me; when he ordered me, to crawl in the back of his squad car" He felt a little twinge at his temple and his mood dampened immediately, as he hesitantly replied, "Aaaaa, Officer Andrews said he didn't think he could hold my kitten and drive. I don't think he has any children of his own." Arnolds' face softened as he considered this. It was an unexpectedly intelligent answer from the old drunk. "By

Golly, that's right!" he said "I can't really keep my eye on Beth and drive myself. Then more loudly he said **"Your Kitten?"** Arnold was now Thinking "What is going on here?"

"Yes replied, Krueger looking down at his feet as if being scolded. He slowly and quietly explained how he had pulled the kitten out of Potters' pond.

After pausing to let that much sink in he went on "I think it wandered off while I was sleeping in the Alley behind Crazy Jacks' Bar and Grill.

Beth followed it back home to me. Arnold could visualize the whole scene and it wasn't pretty. His innocent little curly headed blond angel following a kitten right up to this old drunk, sleeping in one of the most notoriously dangerous corners of town. Sleeping, more likely passed out, in his usual drunken coma. He was just thinking of saying a special prayer to God, for Bills luck in finding Beth, before she came to harm: when Janice yelled up to him. "Honey, Beth and the kitten are sleeping, and I am leaving, I am already half a day late to work!" He gruffly ordered Krueger to hurry up, and take a shower, and get dressed quickly, so they would have time to have a beer and sandwich, before he drove Krueger back to his cardboard box in the alley.

Then he added, as an afterthought, bring your dirty clothes down and I will throw them in the washing machine for you. You can take them in a plastic bag, all nice and clean back to your home. I'll put the bottle of aspirin and another beer in the bag for you. In the end it turned out to be a fortunate exchange for Krueger. Beth's mother, Janice was grateful for the safe return of her daughter. Janice started looking for Krueger on her way home from the clinic with leftover supper, and sometimes warm socks, old shoes, or other items that made his box more comfortable. A couple of years later Courtesy Janice, Krueger had cleaned up and sobered up enough to accept an unofficial position as night security guard and handy man at the clinic, Janice told Dr David, it was easier to have him there at night, than to go looking for him in the dark. Dr David was not happy with the idea, at first, but he never could say no to Janice and after a while he stopped worrying that Krueger would have friends in, or help himself to the prescription pills. Krueger had no friends, with the possible exception of Janice, and was afraid of prescription medications. He wasn't paid; but He had a warm place to stay, where no one bothered him, and three square meals a day. Janice refused to give him money or whiskey; but Dr David made sure he had a meager supply.

Dr David was used to prescribing dangerous prescription medicine, as needed, so it wasn't hard for him to prescribe just the right dose of whiskey to keep

Krueger comfortable but still conscious. Jane's amazing story of Janice and Beth was all news to me, until she got to the point about Krueger being the unofficial night watchman at the clinic. I remembered him. I often saw Krueger when I was Dr David's last patient at the clinic. He was always coming in as I was leaving." I had been listening quietly to Jane's story until she mentioned Krueger and then I said," Oh Yes, I have seen Krueger at the clinic; but I had no idea how he got there or why."

"What has that got to do with Janice filing for a divorce with Arnold?"

"That kitten thing with Beth, was a long time ago and innocent enough"

"Yes", Jane replied," I am coming to that" and continuing her litany of gossip, "that was long ago, and it was an innocent mistake that Beth made then. Cute even. Still she was spoiled even then, and since then, she has gotten into drug use, alcohol abuse, and rumor has it, she even sleeps around, just to upset her parents. Janice and Arnold have paid for the finest baby sitters, tutors and now more recently Beth has stayed at two very expensive rehabilitation clinics. Janice and Arnold have a very nice combined salary but not that nice!"

"I had no idea" I replied. Jane gave me a puzzled look and said, "Well, I just assumed you knew"

"Janice and Arnold have done everything to keep Beth's reputation spotless, but I hadn't thought they had much success." Arnold thinks his little girl can do no wrong, and even though, they have mortgaged their house, and spent their retirement money; Arnold still wants to give his little girl everything she desires. Maybe it is because Janice has seen more damaged lives up close and personal, that she isn't fooled into thinking, Beth can be saved with more money, or anything else she and Arnold have to offer. Janice has said: either Beth straightens up; or the next time she is in trouble, she is on her own, even if it means going to Juvenile detention, or spending the rest of her life in jail."

"Arnold can't – "

With that the conversation ended abruptly, as Arnold's head appeared over the hill.

I reached down to pick up my things and get ready to go, thinking, as I did I will talk to Janice at lunch tomorrow." I worked in the Bank right across the street, and we often had lunch, next door to the Bank, at the Sloppy Joe Diner. "I would find out, how much of Jane's story was true and how much was Fabricated." I thought, "if even half of it is true, Janice has had problems trying to work, and raise a daughter at the same time. I never even suspected. I wish I had known, maybe I could have helped out some way."

The next morning I made an appointment at the clinic with Janice.

I was always having pains in my joints from, not getting enough exercise, and sitting too long in the teller box; so it wasn't hard to come up with an excused to visit the clinic. I knew they wouldn't be busy, as it was Thanksgiving, on Thursday. The patients wouldn't be coming in, for tryptophan comma, with complications, until after they ate the Turkey. Until then the turkeys would be the entertainment in the town of Greenridge for the day.

Janice greeted me, holding open the door and saying, "good morning Mary Darlene, you must really be in pain to come here this early in the morning" "No, I replied, just tired of waking up with pains in my joints," "and I wanted to make a lunch date to talk to you about a rumor I heard" "Rumor about me? That is a new one." Janice replied with a slightly confused look on her face. I was pretty sure, she suspected there was more to it than that. "How about lunch, then?" I said, looking at Janice as she walked me back to Dr David's examination room.

"Today is a light day, you can get away and we can go to that new Chinese restaurant, Dragon's Secret.

I hear that it has high backed booths, that make a little private room to eat in"

"You know me; I never could eat out, without getting half of my dinner, on the front of my blouse." I said all this rapid fire, in one breath. Getting a moment alone with Janice, for idle talk was harder than trying to get a politician to admit he reneged on a campaign promise. Janice gave me a warm chuckle, but she had that familiar expression on her face, that told me she didn't believe a word I said. She wanted to tag along just to see, what I had up my sleeve. Janice was a great help to Dr David. She never ever said, "you were not telling the whole truth;" but by the time she took the patients into Dr David, she had a good idea of the patient's real problems and diagnosis. She could tell which, were genuine symptoms, and which were made up stories to manipulate the Doctor into doing what the patient wanted. It once was just kids that were having trouble in school and wanted to stay home sick: but now it was people wanting prescription drugs. Sometimes, just to, help them to get off street drugs, but often for less noble reasons. I thought," It must be breaking Janice's heart to know the trouble that Beth was in: She knew She and Arnold would not be able to help. Arnold was a fool, not to see that Janice cared just as much, for Beth as he did. He should have understood, that she knew, from experience, that more enabling would only make matters worse." "That sounds like fun Janice replied", helping me up on the exam table and handing me a backless gown to change into." I've been wanting to see the inside of the Secret Dragon myself" How about we meet there at 11 when they open."

Dr. David doesn't have anyone scheduled after 10:30, when Crazy Jack comes in to have his stitches removed. "I heard they have a dish called Schezchuan Shrimp that is hotter than Miss Cory's Cinco de Mayo stuffed Jalapeno peppers," She said over her shoulder, as she left the exam room quietly closing the exam room behind her. I looked at the backless gown thinking, "I hate this thing" "Oh well, it is for a worthy cause" I couldn't wait for Dr David to get thru with my appointment, so I could get back to the bank and tell them I was going to take a 3 hour lunch break to see Doctor David about a pain I was having in my knee.

They didn't need to know, I had already seen Dr David, and had other plans more interesting plans. Dr David gave me a prescription for Naproxen and a paper that said I visited him He wrote exactly what I asked, the day without a time. I had no intention of taking the Naproxen; but I planned to have it filled for Beth, if that was what it took to get her attention. Janice and I both drove up to the Dragon Secret at exactly ten to eleven. "Hi Darlene," Janice said as I groaned my way out of the car. "Didn't the Naproxen help your knees?" "Oh Janice, you notice everything, I haven't gotten the prescription filled yet." "I thought I would wait and take it at bed time, so I could get a good nice sleep for once" I felt a little guilty for lying to Janice, our relationship was based on truth, no matter how ugly. "Well, I consoled myself, half of it was true, and the other half was just a little white lie for an important cause."

Later the restaurant would be the most popular place in town. All the booths would be filled: but this day, it was nearly empty. We picked the most secluded booth in the back of the restaurant. Janice and I had never known anything like it. I noticed she was eying the booths. All the booths were private with high backs and a curtain, that could be pulled to completely obscure the occupants. The waiter indicated we should sit In the booth we had chosen and turned to leave.

Sharing Secrets

"JANICE", I WHISPERED, "Isn't this the perfect place to share secrets?" "This can be our own special secret garden" Janice focused in on me, with those eyes that could find a grain of truth, In a barrel full of lies. "Yes" She said," but it can't be a confessional booth, If I tell you all my secrets, you have to tell me yours." It hadn't occurred to me that I would have to tell all to her all.

The first thing that popped in my head was Janice's husband, Arnold. Then I reasoned, "Arnold wasn't a secret, nothing secret had ever happened between us, He was just a fantasy" I thought of Jose and heard myself saying, "I am in love with a married man" I regretted having said it, before it was completely out of my mouth. Janice's mouth popped open. I sat down quietly in the booth. Janice sat across from me. Nothing ever surprised Janice. She was not easy, for most people to read. Only, because I knew her so well, was I able to see that my secret had shocked her. I steeled myself for the questions I expected to come, but it was as if my secret was one Janice didn't want to know. We sat there silent with our own thoughts, until the waiter brought our orders I couldn't help noticing, as he sat our orders down, this was a feast like none I had seen in a long time. I looked around, and then straight at Janice saying, "We are in a private room at the Secret Dragon, What better place to exchange secrets?"

The waiter sat everything down and pulled the curtain shut. We hadn't known till now, that we would be invited, to enjoy our meal, in the privacy, that was customary in some parts of China. As the waiter pulled the curtain closed, I was already sampling the spicy shrimp. Janice said, "OK, now, what have I done to get talked about, all round town, Talked about, so much, that even you have heard about it? "I was so relieved to be off the hook; I just started blurting out everything, that had been going through my head about Janice and Beth, since Jane relayed her gossip on Green Mountain." It is one thing for you to sacrifice you life, to the service of the town's medical community, and quite another to neglect your daughters' welfare. You are just never able to be there for her." "Wow, I didn't see that coming," Janice said with a terrible expression of remorse on her face. I immediately, regretted having been so blunt. "I am so sorry" I said, "I know you have always done the best you could, for everyone" "I heard a story yesterday, that you filed divorce on Arnold. I couldn't believe it. I just had to confront you and find out the truth for myself." Janice regained her composure immediately. "I am glad you came to me," she said. Then, in her methodically way, She began pouring out her plans to divorce Arnold. You are right, it is because of Beth.

She verified everything, that I had just discovered from Jane. She verified all that I suspected, and even managed to shock me with another fact, I hadn't suspected. Beth was pregnant and she was not sure the father, wasn't Arnold, all sad but true. I was so saddened by her story. It all seemed so unfair. She had given her life to being a good mother, wife, provider and town nurse. It wasn't fair that no one could be Superwoman no matter how hard they tried. She didn't have a full plate, She had an impossible load to bear.

My emotions had surfaced with brief thoughts, of my secret feelings for Janice's husband Arnold, and my eternal love for Jose. I had relaxed, relieved that Janice had temporarily lost interest in my secret. Tears flooded my eyes, and rolled down my cheeks, as she told her story. "Do you really think that Arnold may have gotten

Beth pregnant?" I asked. Janice was quiet for a long time, thinking how to reply. I was beginning to regret my rudeness again, when she replied with finality. "No I don't think so. ""Arnold would rather destroy both of us, than to do anything to harm his precious little girl." "Then equally assertive I replied you need to be, presenting a united front, instead of fighting each other." You need to support each other" Janice replied, "What you say is true, but we can't continue to enable her" I had to admit that she was right. I was to learn that day that tears are every bit as infectious as laughter. Janice told me how hard it had been. She knew from experience, working with drug addicts, that no matter what she tried, she couldn't keep Beth safe. Beth had gone past the point where she could help by being kind. It was time for "tough Love" My emotions had completely escaped me. I cried as she told her story. She was touched by my concern. She wasn't used, to anyone knowing, much less understanding her problem and it was the one thing that could make her burst out in relentless tears.

We sat there on our afternoon out together. We were Not the two unemotional Professional women people had grown to expect. We were just two friends, sharing secrets and crying like babies. Both of us had burst into tears. Later, when I remembered it, I would think of us crying together for hours: but it was more like a minute or two. Janice and I did talk for hours at the Secret Dragon. Once we got going we were like two little girls, sharing secrets in our own club house. As Janice told me about her problems she extracted a promise from me, to tell her all about my secret love. It wasn't till three that Janice glanced at her watch. She had remembered Dr David had a three O'clock appt. She said," I have to get back; Mrs. Adams is coming in to see Dr David at Three. Remember, you promised your secret. Thanksgiving is tomorrow and Dr David and I will be busy with post Turkey dinner syndrome.

Day after tomorrow then?

I WILL MEET you day after tomorrow, same place, same time" "Ohmygosh, I replied, they will never believe me at the bank, when I tell them, that I was in Dr David's office all day" I said as I added my money to the tray, for the bill, and hurried out. Janice was close behind me on the way to her car. "Tell her you were helping me with a cookie list for Beth's school ", she said. "Beth is not really interested in selling them this year. I could care less and don't have time." "OK, I said with a fake grimace, but if I get fired for selling cookies at the bank, you better have a spot waiting for me with Dr David.

Janice broke into one of her sunny smiles and said, "Don't I wish you needed a job. I will have three spots waiting for you, all with long hours and short pay. "I will pick up the cookie order list tomorrow, when we meet to tell secrets." I replied, as I drove off in a hurry. The day at the Bank was as boring as usual, but It passed quickly. Thinking about possible ways to help Arnold and Janice save their wayward teen had occupied my mind. I really had no time to be bored with the usual squabbles and problems of tellers with customers making impossible requests. The recession had brought with it personal financial problems that everyone wanted someone else to solve for them. I was the Bank Manager, and all the "sticky wicky" ended up square on top of my desk.

More than once, the thought, that I should change the placard on my door to read "Complaint Department," instead of Bank Manager. My little personal joke had relaxed my own tension enough, more than once, so that I was able to sooth the ruffled feathers of customers who were angry their pay checks wouldn't cover their expenses. I was given credit for performing miracles by tellers frustrated, with trying to explain what the impoverished clients would not hear. I was pleased to accept the praise but knew full well it was just a matter of repeat, repeat repeat before the clients finally had to give up and accept the truth. The tellers did the real work, sorting out the problems, before they dropped them and the client in my office. The tellers, did for me, what Janice did for Dr David when she took the patients to the examining room. The day at the Bank passed so quickly, I had no time to be bored. I had forgotten Jose and my private life completely. The day was pretty uneventful. No one complained the bank had stolen their money.

It seemed that I had no sooner walked in, when it was already time to set the time lock on the vault, and leave for the day When I arrived home, I remembered the letter, I had mailed to Jose that morning. I popped a TV dinner in the microwave and mused. "Maybe I could solve our problem and Beth's at the same time.

"Jose has the perfect place to stay while Beth has her baby. Janice and Dr David could arrange the delivery and stay at Jose's Restaurant. Jose and I could marry. It would be easy enough for Jose and I, to claim the baby was ours and return in a few months, with Jose the new citizen, and Beth "our maid" and baby makes four. I chuckled to myself, from alone in an empty house to instant family of four. Beth's baby would be our secret little story of Moses.

It all seemed perfectly natural to me. "Everyone cares about their birth parent; I however, never could understand what it was all about." With that thought, I realized how tired I was. I dropped my empty TV tray in the trash and went to the refrigerator to get a bottle of cherry crème soda for desert. My TV dinner, came from the freezer, and I always had water from the cooler with my meals.

There, staring at me was the half thawed Turkey, I had promised to cook for tomorrow's turkey dinner. Abigail Ester was a cousin, on the Freedman side of the family. She graduated from Lincoln High that year in June. She had worked at the same Alpha Beta, as I had many years ago. She worked as I had to save up money for the Bus ticket to Greenridge. The High School counselor was a young black woman I had never met. She had heard of me. She put Abigail in touch with me. When Abigail wrote and asked for my help. I offered her an entry level job at the bank. I found her a small apartment to rent.

Abigail had just settled in and didn't yet have many friends. I had invited her to my house for Thanksgiving dinner. I bought the Turkey and all the fixings to prepare, before the Hike up Green Mountain. I made cranberry sauce. I put the turkey in the refrigerator to thaw that night, after the hike. I set my alarm for 5 AM so I could clean and cook the Turkey for dinner. Then I took a shower and went to bed. Abigail arrived at 11 AM. She was eager to please and genuinely impressed with my apartment and position as manager of the local Bank. She talked enthusiastically about being in the big city, but I detected a hint of homesick-ness. She came from a large loving family Their Thanksgiving dinner was probably much more modest than my own.

Still, it was her family, and her home. To a young woman that had never been on her own before, home for the holidays was the place to be. Over dinner, she talked about home, and I gave her my opinions on the "Perfect Teller" and helped her set small goals to improve her future with the bank she helped clear the table and we did the dishes together. I was glad, when she excused herself and left. As I closed the door behind her, I wondered to myself. "She seems so young" "I am getting old and set in my ways." The thought passed quickly as the phone rang and Jose was on the other end.

Dreaming up a solution

WE TALKED OF our love for each other, and our longing to make it work, now that everyone that opposed us as a couple was gone. At first I just listened and we went over the same problems, we had gone over and over before. Then we talked of his home and restaurant. He was always hosting big family gatherings, which only reminded him, that he had been deserted, and left alone by his wife and children. I told him about my hike up Green Mountain, the story I heard from Jane. The gossip that was more than verified by Janice at the Secret Dragon. Then more as a funny story, or a joke; I told him the "solution" I had dreamed up, to solve all of Janice, Beth's and Jose's problems. I was surprised when he said "It just might work" "If you and Janice decide tomorrow to try it, call me and I will get busy working things out on my end." He said "I would like being a proud father again. What about your reputation as Bank Manager? Aren't you supposed to be above reproach?" He did have a point, but I simply replied, "Yes, but I think I am allowed to be human" He said "Till tomorrow then, call me after you get home. I can't wait to hear what Janice thinks of your solution" I went to bed, happy to be planning with Jose, but wishing, I hadn't promised Janice to tell her my secret life the next day. I tried to think of ways I could have avoided disclosing everything, but there just wasn't any. Janice had said, "I am not confessing, we are sharing secrets" and of course she was right. Where could I begin? What could I say to make her understand how I felt? She was the perfect white woman, raised in Camelot. She had been sent to the finest schools and was without blemish. I was the complete Opposite. I feared that the "love of my life", would be nothing but a sordid affair, in her eyes. The next morning the alarm rang a full five minutes before I reluctantly dragged myself out of bed to get ready and go to work. The next morning was a nightmare. Not only were their two angry clients waiting in my office but because the computers had crashed It was not possible to obtain information from their accounts or any others. The Computers were accepting routine deposits and withdrawals, but I feared that the business we did and the information we entered might not all be there, when the computers came back on line. I insisted that everyone keep complete written records. You would have thought I had asked the tellers to tear down the old bank, and rebuild it from scratch. I suppose, in a way, that is exactly how they felt. We had to find the old hand written forms or create new ones in their place. Abigail surprised me by jumping right in, and really doing a great job creating and filling in forms for the other tellers. She had no preconceived ideas of how things should run, so was quick to learn how to make the system work and run with it.

The next morning Janice rang me between patients We agreed to meet at our Secret Dragon Garden for lunch. Things had just started to make some sense, when I glanced at the clock and realized it was time for me to meet Janice at the Secret Dragon. When I pulled up at the Secret Dragon, Janice's car was already there. She had gone in and taken our table. She was just ordering as I walked up and sat down. "Oh thank goodness", she said "I was afraid you had forgotten all about our date in the secret garden." I was still feeling very reluctant, and sorry I had promised to tell my secrets, but answered. "Oh you know, just another, one of those days from hell, at the Bank.

All our computers decided to take the day off" Janice had finished ordering and the waiter turned to me with "What will you have?" "I will have the spicy shrimp again, they were so good""Excellent choice", He replied and left to put in our order. While we were waiting for our meal and time alone, Janice made me laugh with stories of her many patients that had overdone Thanksgiving. I, in turn, told her about my dinner with Abigail and how well she was catching on at the bank. The waiter had no sooner sat down our plates, and shut our curtain, when Janice turned to me with a wink and a grin and said. "Oh! You are the sly sneaky one" "You have got to tell me absolutely everything, about your secret love life." I took a deep breath and said," I don't know how to begin but," "You remember the Jackson family?"

They were just starting up the new Sizzler, a year or so, after I started working at the Bank. "I was young and so eager." Abigail reminds me, of who I was back then." Anyway I made this deal with them. They would take me with them, on their vacation to Mexico. I would show them how to set up an accounting system for their new business. We were both so inexperienced. Neither of us realized; we were way in over our heads. Still, somehow we managed, and none of the things I had overlooked, ever came back to haunt us. Beginners luck, I guess. That is where I met Jose Gutierrez, the love of my life. Janice was all ears. She looked at me dreamily, as she said, "I do

remember your going to Mexico with the Jackson family"
You were there for most of the summer.

When you finally came back your looked radiant."
I should have realized immediately, that the glow was
more than just a sun tan, but the thought never entered
my head." "Go on, go on" I related the whole story of my
romance with Jose and the roadblocks we encountered.
I had misjudged Janice Her eyes shone with excitement
at mention of my love of Jose and she was sad and
disappointed when I had told her why we had only just
been good friends for all these years. Encouraged by her
positive response, I wound up by jokingly mentioning
the crazy solution, to all our problems I had "come up
with" Let's do it! Janice didn't think it was funny at all.
She seemed not to notice, that I had said it was a joke.
"We have got to make this work!" was her enthusiastic
reply. Janice's face went from on the verge of tears to
open mouthed with awe. She was obviously relieved,
and her only comment was, "Oh if only we can make it
work" Encouraged again by her enthusiasm, I replied I
didn't know, but I was sure going to give it my best effort.
She looked ten years younger and her face shone as she
replied," me too." I could see she was ready to take off
running with my "solution" "OK" I said," but not today" I
had glanced at my watch. I could see, we were both going
to be very late getting back from lunch. Considering the

mess that was waiting for me at the Bank, I was almost as sorry to leave our lunch date, as I had been to come. "OK," then she said "Tomorrow, same place, same time to work out the details." The third day we met again, as planned, at our secret garden. This time we met to finish making plans, for our secret solution. We would take Beth to Mexico to have her baby" That would not be for at least another six months. First we had to keep the pregnancy secret. We also had to make sure Beth's health care needs were met, and she graduated with her class from High School.

First, we had to enlist Beth's cooperation. Jane, the gossipy neighbor, unwittingly was a big help with that, because of her, Beth was anxious to move in with me. Jane, their watchful next door neighbor had eyed her one afternoon as she came back from school and asked "are you gaining a little weight, Beth ?" "I declare that jumper outfit fits you tighter than it used to." Beth, always quick to think on her feet replied, "Yes, the cotton was made in Indonesia. I think it shrank a little in the wash, Besides, I am on my period and you know how that is." Jane replied, "Indeed I do." Her face said she still suspected there was more to it than that. After that little encounter, Beth was anxious to move in with me. "Are you sure she will agree to live with me till then as my cook and housekeeper?" I said as I unlocked my car door. "Oh yes, I am sure"

Janice replied." She later relayed what Jane had said to Beth that morning. Pulling her own car door open she continued, "She needs credit, for future employment class to graduate next year" "Besides what else can she do to take an unnoticed year off from school when she begins to show."

"You can help her with that""I seem to remember you still weren't showing, the week before you delivered Beth full term" I said as I slammed the door behind me and started my car engine. "And you think I can convince her to eat what I tell her to?" Janice said, as that tearful expression flashed across unfamiliar territory, on her face, and was immediately gone. She stepped on it and raced her sleek blue car out of the parking lot." I followed slowly in my new black Mercedes. I was sure Janice wouldn't have any problem, persuading Beth to follow the diet she recommended, once I clued in "Little Miss Clueless" as to whose reputation was about to be smeared, and whose popularity was going down the tubes ;if, or rather when the truth came out. We had planned the perfect way out for her. I had no doubt she would go for it, If only I could approach her, and the subjects very slowly and carefully. The trick was to make friends with her. I was already consulting my knowledgeable friends, and co workers on how to manage that. If I could just keep her from bolting like a skittish horse at first sight of me, I was sure I would have no problem making her see the light. As it turned out, all my planning to persuade Beth to work with us, was unnecessary. Thanks to Jane and some sly glances from her classmates, She was already starting to consider how she would get through her senior year, without arousing suspicion. Fortunately, dropping out, was not an option she even considered. I returned to the Bank, expecting the worse, but by then the computers were back up, and we were starting to check the data that we collected, with the data that was entered when the computers were down. The rest of the afternoon went smoothly and I was already thinking about our meeting with Beth the next day at our favorite secret garden. I called Jose as soon as I got home from work. Warming up some leftover turkey, as I dialed his number. We talked for hours. He was excited about the whole idea. I guess you could say I proposed to him, and he accepted, with all the conditions, I was trying to work out. I wondered why it had taken me so long to speak my mind. I think Jose felt the same way. Before dashing back to work, we agreed to bring Beth to our Secret Dragon Garden to make her a willing participant in our plan, to join our two families and add two more members. Janice knew Beth's soft spot and let her skip school the next day to spend the day with us. We all met at the Secret Dragon for lunch and Beth was easy to persuade. She had already considered the problems she would have trying to go to school with a new baby on the way. Janice drove off a little more slowly than usual, because Beth was with her, and she was thinking how she could persuade Dr David to accept, an all expense paid fishing vacation to Mexico to deliver Beth's baby. She knew he would be reluctant to leave the young intern in charge, for even a short time: but her emergency would give him the iron clad excuse, to take the week off and enjoy the fishing trip he had dreamed of for so long. I followed in my car, thinking," what a lovely young mother and daughter" Janice and Beth were, It was very fortunate that Beth had completed most of the classes she needed to earn her degree in Business Math All she needed were the two accounting classes she had already signed up for. Who better to help her with that, than me? Our next step was to convince Miss Tendry the accounting teacher to let her do the work with her maid duties, at my house and allow me to deliver the assignments and supervise her progress. Miss Tendry, the accounting teacher of Beth's class was a knock out. She was up on latest teenager's fashions. Barely, more than a teenager herself, she was the most popular teacher at Beth's school and owed me a favor. I had helped her plan a lesson that involved a visit to the Bank. Time to collect the favor, I thought, as I drove into bank parking and turned my thought to explaining, why I was coming in late to work again.

I always tried to eat light as, I got little exercise and gained weight easily. Janice insisted she shop with me and we not buy anything more than usual, in the way of fattening foods. She stocked us up on fresh fruit and vegetables. My habit of popping a TV dinner in the oven came to a screeching halt. Janice spent her lunch break, at my house counseling Beth on her duties; which Janice decided including fixing a proper meal for Beth and myself. Beth didn't start showing until we all left for our Mexican Vacation. I lost weight and felt better than I had in a long long time. I even started making it all the way to the top of Green Mountain on our club meetings. Jane commented on how good I looked and I thanked her and smiled. She was going to suspect the baby, we came back with from Mexico wasn't mine; but she could think what she liked. We definitely couldn't let her in on the secret, without telling the whole town, and that would not do. Janice and I had both worked long and hard at our boring hum drum jobs.

Now we were thick as thieves, and our scheming in the Secret Dragon Garden, brought more real excitement to our day to day existence than any clandestine love affair every could have. Beth had her own room and enough of childish behavior. She settled in, and grew up faster than either of us could have hoped for. She took a real fancy to accounting, and I was beginning to think that she would make a first rate part time employee at the bank, as soon as the baby was old enough for Kindergarten. I wasn't going to mention that to her. The "Maid service" was just too good, to want to give up. It included the laundry, dusting and a wonderful home cooked meal every evening. Janice and I mostly did the laundry and dusting together; but that home cooked meal really made my day. Janice monitored everything with an occasional visit to Dr David. Everyone was looking forward to the vacation in Mexico. Beth was a little nervous, but everything went very well. Time passed quickly. It seemed to me that no time had passed at all before, we were all on the plane to Mexico. Janice and I took three months off. Dr David waited till the due date to leave his intern in charge. The baby cooperated nicely by arriving the day after he arrived in Mexico. Jose was best friend of the local police chief and minister. The wedding and birth certificates were all ready to be signed when we arrived. "Our baby" attended the wedding, that we held in Jose's Inn, along with many of Jose's friends. Everyone knew of our love and after all I was a "crazy American Women "The same rules didn't apply to me as to the local Senoritas.

Dr David got the best fishing equipment and guide, all arranged by Jose; before we arrived. Dr David would tell stories of his wonderful fishing vacation, until his retirement. For all I know, he may be telling them still.

Jose will be getting his citizenship next week. We bought Jane's big house next door, to Arnold and Janice. Jose and Arnold are best friends. Jose built a Mexican restaurant on the edge of town. Janice and I still prefer our private room at the Secret Dragon for lunch. Lately, we have been joking, about whether we should buy Beth and the baby an RV, or just build a big tunnel between our two houses, as Beth and Baby are always en route from one house to the other. Between Janice, Jose and Beth I am dining like a Queen I am having no more problems with my weight or my knees. But still, the thing I appreciated the most, was the day Beth looked lovingly at me and said. "What everyone needs is a good mother in law"

Bobby survives

DR GORDON EXAMINED Bobby ahead of Mrs. Ludlow but by the time, he had sent Bobby to X-Ray, Mrs. Ludlow was actually feeling much better. From X-Ray Bobby went straight to surgery. He was personally escorted, by Mrs. Jackson, all the way. He was out of the Recovery room, and admitted into a regular hospital room in record time. Marcie Jackson allowed Amber to miss school so that she could be at Bobby's side. The Jackson and Williams families, found themselves becoming fast friends, in spite of their wishes to the contrary.

Getting together, How the circle came together

MARY DARLENE STARTED a search for answers to child rearing and social ethics Problems, because of Beth. It wasn't long before she discovered the Ethics meetings and became a regular attendee Mary Darlene, Beth and Janice included the accounting teacher in an occasional dinner at the Secret Dragon Miss Tendry, Accounting teacher talked to Mary Darlene and Janice about her afternoon study group for last year High School students. She, the Math teacher, Mr. Lattimar and the history teacher Mr. Ludlow held the afternoon study class to make accounting, math and history. More relevant for the students of their classes. The students were allowed to ask questions. Sometimes, spontaneous questions, asked in class became the focus of the afternoon study Groups. The study group was very successful and later became the Ethics Club Mr. Ludlow is only ten years younger than Mary Beth He is blond with bronze tanned complexion. He always dresses in tie, sweater vest, tweed pants and coat. He, at first appears quite scholarly, but on second glance is active and well built. It was pretty obvious to Mary Darlene and Janice that Miss Tendry, the accounting teacher has a big crush on him. His wife died only a year after he signed on as History teacher, to care for his ill wife and his two boys. Mr. Ludlow had published many of his archeology finds in journals He was a distinguished and well known scholar with tenure privileges at the University of Texas. He gave it all up to accept a job at the local high school to care for his ill wife and young teen age boys.

The Ethics Club

MR. LUDLOW STAR-
TED the after school
history club with the accounting teacher The club's
interest included, mathematics of ancient economics and
accounting practices. Ancient economics were compared
to modern methods of accounting. Mr. Ludlow's
history class supplied a complete history of ancient
methods of accounting. Miss Tendry's accounting class,
was responsible for researching modern methods and
Comparing the ancient methods, to modern ones, with
the help of Mr. Lattimer's Algebra's class. Mr. Lattimer
was the oldest of the group He had long white hair. He
had been at the High School since its opening in 1942.
No one seemed to know his real age, or care, but he was
definitely well over whatever number, might come to

mind. In addition to Mathematics he also taught music and conducted the local orchestra and band. He was in great shape for an octagerian, or whatever plus, and would walk alongside the band when they were on parade. The very "Butch" gymnastics teacher, Miss Irene Flank, shared responsibility for the band and orchestra with Mr. Lattimer. "Miss Irene" was responsible for marching practice and discipline of the band members. If students had problems, they went to Lattimer. If their behavior was not up to school standards they were sent to see Miss Irene. Miss Irene had been a marine drill Sergeant and she saw active combat with her trainees. When she left the Marines she took classes in gymnastics, physical education, and physical therapy.

She lacked the sympathy with people in pain to be a physical therapist. Discipline was her forte. Miss Irene taught both the boys and girls gym classes, as well as, coaching the football team for the school.

Mr. Ludlow had been on an archeological team at the University of Texas. He had traveled the world, searching for Ancient secrets. His travels included Ireland looking for the "little people" (vegetarians who lived in harmony with nature and vanished into the forest when Roman legions arrived. Eventually, they were wiped out by the men with the Iron swords that came from Rome. They lived in Glass houses, which were burned to the ground, by the men of the iron swords. Occasional fine silver swords or goblets and fantastic crystal ware were found, but no written record of their existence exists. Only myths of banshees and fairies. He followed the Anasazi Indians (ancient ones) thru New Mexico and Utah, visiting the energy vortexes of the Grand Canyon Mr. Ludlow deciphered hieroglyphs on cave walls of hunting Cro-Magnon men. He searched for trace evidence of the survivors of Atlantians in Egypt, and researched the Aborigine natives of the Australian Outback. He had a deep interest, not only in recorded, but pre recorded history, as well. He wanted nothing less than to open the secrets of ancient civilizations. The teachers met for a potluck dinner, rotating their homes. It gave them a chance to prepare for the next club meeting with the students. After Mary Darlene joined the group, the Pot luck turned into a Gourmet dinner prepared by the host/hostess,

Mary Darlene and Jose

MARY DARLENE'S HUSBAND, Jose, joined to improve his English and get some, "alone time" with Mary Darlene, away from Beth and the Baby. Jose had first one and then two restaurants. It soon became the practice of the group, to share expenses for dinner at Jose's. Jose was interested in listening to the teachers discussions and, later, joining in on the rituals they practiced. He did not have an aptitude, or interest in preparing lessons for the students. Jose did the Cooking. He also set up the private back room in one of his restaurants, for the meetings to prepare lessons. He did not attend any of the class meetings with the students. Jose had met Major Paulina and Mary Jane when they were on furlough.

How Major Paulina and Mary Jane became acquainted with Jose and Mr. Ludlow

MAJOR PAULINA AND Mary Jane spent their furlough researching the Santeria culture in Mexico. Jose had been their guide, as well as host, at the Inn, where they stayed for three months. Jose became fast friends with the two of them and Major Paulina's daughter Janice. Jose knew nothing of "the cone" the powerful secret project Major Paulina and Mary Jane were working on. Janice also had no inkling of the military purpose behind her mother's interest in magic. The original name of the assisted Cone was ELORA, or Electromagnetic Ohmn Resonance Amplifier Paulina, her daughter Janice, and Mary Jane were among the few people Jose knew that lived near Greenfield, when he married and moved in with Mary Beth. It was only natural that he would introduce them to his new group of friends at the club meetings. Mr. Ludlow was immediately interested in Mary Jane's Paulina's knowledge and practice of witchcraft and they, soon joined the dinner club at Jose's.

Getting it all together

J ANICE JOINED THE dining group at Jose's restaurants. She was seldom able to make any of the club meetings at the High School. Beth occasionally attended either, or both, the club meeting at the school and the dinner meeting afterwards. After she graduated from high school, she had the baby to care for. She was also taking accounting courses, sponsored by Mary Darlene and the Bank. She worked part time weekends at the Bank and wanted to follow in Mary Darlene's footsteps with a banking career. She fainted at the sight of blood and had no interest in the medical profession.

Ancient use of circle magic is introduced to the club by Paulina

THE CONE WAS introduced to the Ethics club with Paulina's help. Paulina, Mary Jane and Mr. Ludlow had a great deal of knowledge of Ancient secrets of energy and matter manipulation. Mr. Ludlow's class introduced the Ethics club to the many ways that religion, at one time, was not separated from government. Laws were made by religious leaders and enforced by government leaders. Sometimes, the law makers and enforcers were one and the same. Religion had been used to solve the dilemmas of the ethics of economic and social interactions.

He reported on a Witches' Conference. The Witches attended the conference by riding on brooms, or if unable to attend physically they attended astrally, with the aide of flying ointment, and a circle or unassisted cone. The student's report brought on many questions. The students were anxious to pursue the Questions in the Ethics club. The more answers that were given by Mr. Ludlow, the more questions showed up. Finally, it was decided the club would research and design a ritual containing a circle for a worthwhile goal. The purpose of the first circle was to travel in time and space

The Ethics Club students take over the Ethics club

THE ETHICS CLUB wanted to see for themselves many of the things they were reading about in their history books. They visited many of the same places that Mr. Ludlow had visited and told them about, as they studied the lands he had visited.

They wanted to understand, what happened in the past, in those strange lands. Their flying trips were very successful, and led to a new enthusiasm for history. History gave them many answers to what caused problems and poverty and what solutions might be possible to solve them. The High School students, soon pointed out that, they wanted not only to study.

Possibilities, but to put them to use. Mary Jane, Paulina and Mr. Ludlow had not intended to introduce Wiccan magic to the Ethics Club. They could not deny it had been much more successful, than they had intended. Many dinners after the club meetings were devoted more to the ethics of teaching ancient religions than to actually planning, the ethics club meetings Paulina, Jose and Mr. Ludlow thought that is was very ill conceived and even dangerous, to allow High School student access to ancient secrets, especially any that were concerned with religions other than the more accepted Christian or Hebrew ones.

Mr. Ludlow said one night, over one of Jose's excellent turtle soups, "It is quite one thing to acquaint the students with exotic dishes, such as this fine soup, even eating grasshoppers and termites is acceptable, but to teach religious practices other than those recognized in our community, already is forbidden fruit." We simply can't allow any such practices to be remotely connected with the school's reputation." "There are guidelines even for what subjects may be presented, even for what books the school library may carry."

Mary Jane and Mr. Lattimer were equally determined that they should allow the students to pursue their questions and come up with solutions to their problems.

"Now just consider this Mr. Ludlow" "These very High School students you and their parents want to protect from cruel reality are on the verge of stepping off the tower of education and falling to their doom. They are ill prepared to face the economic and social problems our generation has left them."

"They will soon step off and hit the cold cruel world with a bang."

"I am not sure there is any hope for the future, but I for one am willing to let them find it, no matter how unconventional it is."

"They are our only hope, meager as it is." I think the possibility of their and our survival as a nation is more important than anyone's reputation. "Mary Darlene chimed in with "I really don't have a right to say this as I have nothing to gain or lose with the school's reputation, but I think everyone knows what I think of pomp and circumstance, and if they don't let me just say I don't give a fig or a fiddly-damn for anyone's reputation." Jose's turned dark, as he looked across the table at Mary Darlene. He well understood the roadblocks that society had put out for Mary Darlene. He changed sides in less time than it took his face to return to its' normal color. She made it look easy as she flew over the hurdles, but he well knew, it was anything but easy for her. In the end, it was Mr.

Lattimer that won the arguments over Mr. Ludlow, Miss Tendry, Jose, and Paulina.

Many successes of the Ethic club, in circle and many discussion of the proper use, or even knowledge of secret powers, prompted Pauline and Mary Jane, to tell of their secret military project, to Jose and Mr. Ludlow. They told them at one of the after club, dinner discussions of the proper place, versus the misuse of ancient secrets. Paulina, related how she had used the assisted cone in much the same way the Ethics Club had used the unassisted Cone for travel thru time and space. She went on to tell them how much it had troubled her, that she had been unable to develop The instrument to assist the cone without accepting money from the government. She had felt that if she did not complete its development someone else would. She felt that if any government should have it, then it should be the American government. She felt she had a responsibility to see the power was used properly for good and not misused for selfish purposes and she felt with the government giving her the money she might not be able to fulfill that responsibility. The first use of the ELORA developed by Paulina, was by Pauline, to travel to ancient sites of power. She had visited many of the that Paulina and Mr. Ludlow had visited in their travels, but with the cone they were able to visit them in another time. Then when a hurricane off the coast of California was expected to rage thru their small town she decided to ride the wind of a hurricane and create a bubble to deflect it from the Middletown area.

The Ethics class uses the cone

PAULINE AND MARY Jane had changed the name from Paulina's original ELORA to the Circular Transporter Beam. They just called it the Cone or CTB so the Senators wouldn't waste everyone's time by trying to understand the scientific principles implied by the original name.

They had agreed to use the ELORA designed by Pauline. Paulina had originally hoped to build the ELORA, without sharing her ideas with the military. Paulina explained all this to those at the dinner after the Ethics Club meeting. She explained how her concerns and why she had initially been against any experimentation in ancient arts by such young students. She had not even wanted the military to know the secrets that she and Mr. Ludlow had long ago uncovered. The CTB made the misuse of that power much more dangerous. She rightly feared the power would fall into the wrong hands. She explained with tears in her eyes, She did not have enough money herself to complete the CTB. She was forced to build it at the Stone Mountain Military Base. She had been very successful in using it. It wasn't long before the military was envious of her success in downgrading the hurricane off the California Coast, that threatened to wipe out Middletown and its' neighbors.

Paulina could not make General Whunsch understand that not any group of minds could control the powerful cone produced with the ELORA's assistance. Senator Gross had demanded satisfaction for the thousands of dollars, the government had poured into the project. He insisted on being witness to, and part of the project. He imagined it was similar to the transporter beam of Star Trek fame.

Mary Darlene thought that came pretty close to the truth, given his background. It is suppose to be Top Secret, of course She continued. – "We have done Astral Projection together. "Gone Flying" together as witches did long before the burning times." "The astral body is a higher vibration than the physical. It was easy for me to selectively pick it up, as I put up a cone." "Surrounding myself with it as always, but this time with the help of the circular Transporter Beam"

She gestured around the table as she continued, "All of you and the others in our group that have been putting up a cone with the aide of our circle, on Green Mountain." "It was easy enough for us to achieve unity of purpose and mind" "It's what makes our spells, and prayers, work."

The military immediately recognized the power I produced alone with a CTB assisted cone," "I explained that my power could be multiplied 100 times by having twelve others, like myself in the circle. I had our group in mind. I wasn't ready to say so until I received unanimous group approval."

"Colonel Gross immediately took over my project, selecting Senator Beard, who has supported his Military projects by getting congress to allocate funds, and His own personnel staff. No way would he hear of allowing civilian Adepts to be privy of the CTB. All my arguments against controlling the cone by individuals, with no experience in controlling energy; Allowing such inexperienced, non adepts to attempt to control such a thing with their undisciplined minds,

I maintained was very dangerous and unwise. All my arguments fell on deaf ears. They had been present when I erected a cone of power and directed it. They thought the energy of the CTB could be harnessed by anyone, which is partially true.

The Disaster

THE ENERGY WAS less when I used it alone. It also appeared to them, to be very benign."

"I anticipated that their greed for power would warp the cone and misdirect it. I like you, thought it would just fail; because they would lack unanimity of purpose. At worst, I thought they might all get a fierce sick headache. I don't like to contemplate such things, as I know negativity attracts negativity on the spiritual plane. I was tired and went into a severe depression.

I was no longer happy with myself for having designed the cone in the first place. I could see I had run up against a brick wall trying to persuade the Colonel to allow Adepts to manage the cone. It was becoming obvious that Colonel Gross wanted to use the power of the CTB as a weapon of aggression. It took more patience than I had. I could do nothing. I could not even control my emotions I was depressed, because I knew I should have known they would seek to use the CTB as a weapon, before I accepted their help in building the CTB in the first place. I had enormous feelings of guilt for having designed the CTB in the first place

I fainted from overwork and frustration. The military Doctor, they took me to, decided that I had a severe bout of the flu. I took a long overdue furlough, in lieu of sick leave. It was an unforgivable neglect of responsibility on my part. I lost my will and focus. I allowed control of my creation to slip from my hands." Mary Jane looked puzzled for the first time. She of course, knew of Paulina's success but not of her troubled conscience or of the terrible disaster that had occurred She could not imagine Paulina with a weakened spirit or Will under any circumstances.

Up till now when she had decided to ask for the group's help, Paulina had spared Mary Jane the details of the terrible tragedy that had occurred. Now Mary Jane could imagine the immense pressure, Paulina had been under, but even so. Paulina was anything, but weak. She simply nodded and spoke up with more force and volume than she had intended, "You certainly can't blame yourself for having a weakened spirit or will!!" I have never met anyone with a stronger will!" This time everyone looked at Mary Jane and nodded their approval.

Pauline's demeanor softened as she paused and looked at Mary Jane's still puzzled expression.

She simply said, "No You have never seen me at my lowest. The minute I left for furlough, my condition improved.

It is true that The furlough lifted my spirit and restored my will; but at a terrible expense."

Again making a sweeping gesture to the whole group, She continued ; "You remember: We traveled as a group to exorcise the distraught spirit of Devil's Run in West Virginia. The immense relief and joy that working with our group of "like minded" individuals and the success Of our ritual was short lived."

"You also must remember I was summoned back early from my furlough It was because of the tragedy."

"We read about it in the Newspaper. *Disappeared* was a cover up used for the unrecognizable mess that was found. The sole remains of their bodies." Mary Jane sucked in her breath and uttered an almost inaudible, "Ohh""How terrible" Most of the others at the table, simply gaped in shock. Mr. Ludlow and Mr. Lattimer showed concern but little surprise. Major Paulina cast a brief glance of concern in Mary Jane and Miss Tendry's direction and continued. "Senator Beard and Colonel Gross had papers drawn up in my absence, assigning the project to themselves and their trusted crews. They proceeded, post haste to attempt what they had witnessed me Do, the minute I was out of sight." I don't know, if they had even agreed on a unanimous goal, before they erected the cone. I had explained ; that it would be necessary. Perhaps, they had; but either, consciously or unconsciously, they gave the cone, multiple, negative directions with disastrous consequences, or so it appeared to me." "Probably, no one will ever know exactly what they did, or were thinking, when they did it."

"After the tragedy, when I was summoned back from my furlough to report immediately; It was all over." Senator Beard, Colonel Gross and their most trusted crews were a fused and partially cremated mess. There was little left of the Bunker they had used. The CTB itself was outside the cone, and unharmed." "It was reported that they mysteriously disappeared" "The military still has no idea why the original project burnt to the ground. "I was called to the Pentagon, and asked to explain, why the tragedy had occurred. General Whunssh demanded I set up safety measures and guidelines to keep it from occurring again."

"Fortunately, my original objection to having military personnel and non-adepts rather than Adepts control the cone had gone on record."

"The high ranking military I spoke with could not accept the principles of mind control of the cone. They had been initially impressed with Colonel Gross and Senator Beard's report of the power of the CTB assisted cone. They attributed it all to the CTB and could not quite grasp the concept of mind control of the energies of the cone. Now, because of the accident, they were even more determined to have the CTB. They had no other explanation for the "accident" and so agreed to restore my control and allow the adepts of my choice to control the cone, so long as none of them were privy to the physics behind the CTB. Paulina finished relating the story of her secret project with the military and her request for the assistance of the Ethics Club. It seemed ironic, that she had opposed the High School Students study of unconventional methods, and religions, and was now suggestion they take on, a military developed power that had already destroyed a number of seasoned veteran soldiers and prominent congressional aides, not to mention Senator Beard himself. The dinner club finished eating in silence. They congratulated Jose on his exceptional culinary skills and left quietly for their transportation.

It took several more dinner meetings, before the students questioning in class and in the ethics club and their continuing enthusiasm for finding solutions to very real current problems as well as their successes in circles and researching ancient magic on their own persuaded, the after dinner group in charge, to allow a circle to be held on the Stone Military Base with the assistance of Paulina's cone. The purpose of their first circle with the CTB was debated. They wanted a worthwhile cause the students would be able to support as one mind. It shouldn't be something, that was motivated by greed. The simple desire for all of them to get a high paying job after high school was immediately ruled out. The students were told that they would be holding the circle in a place of great power. It was not possible to let them know more. As with the circles on Green Mountain their parents' permission had to be obtained for a "School outing"

The assisted Cone

PAULINA WAS WAIT-
ING anxiously for Mary
Jane's arrival. She greeted her with, "I am so glad you
were able to come with so little sleep after your last shift.
I wanted to talk to you before we put up the first assisted
cone."

We haven't had a chance to talk, since we asked the
Ethics Club for help in controlling the CTB. I related
something to the whole Club that you had not heard
before. What did you think of my confessional? Mary
Jane related her feelings on the meeting, and Paulina's
confession to the Ethics dinner Group. Mary Jane was
not surprised at the force of Paulina's persuasive powers.
She was surprised that Pauline had felt weakened enough
to lose control of her will for even a brief second. She

said she wished that Paulina had let her share her worries more but she was thinking that she didn't know if she would have been able to hold up under the pressure. The night of the ritual at the Stone Mountain Military Base Mary Jane was the first to arrive after Paulina. She had left from work only a few hours earlier.

She and Paulina were now watching the CTB around the clock. Seldom did they get time off together. Everyone but Mary Jane had been briefed on the circle and the purpose that had been chosen for their first assisted cone. Mary Jane went on to confess to Paulina that she had been shocked by her reaction to the news of the terrible tragedy and its circumstances. The news had allayed her fears. "Now, she thought, I don't have to worry about the unnatural setting. Paulina has everything under control." Aloud she said," I'm impressed." I know you said we would be using the instrument you had designed to increase the power of the cone. I really hadn't grasped your meaning. I also understand, now, why we have to erect the cone here."

"Are you afraid the military will bring charges against you for the deaths and damage caused by the first cone?"

"No, Mary Jane, I am not." Major Paulina replied with conviction.

"I hope you never have to deal with the way they think. I fear you will, and all too soon. We all have to deal with it. It has brought me no joy."

Quickly, changing the subject. Paulina said "Dljaina, the Priestess for tonight's ceremony has already explained the purpose of tonight's cone to you? "Vaguely", Mary Jane replied." Will you go over it with me." Major Pauline began with what Mary Jane thought she was probably the last person in the circle to find out. "My daughter, the young Priestess Janice, wants to have a love child with her James. Today, we are calling the Archangel Gabriella and Father Sky to ask them for aide in directing the energies of the planets conjunct with the Moon to Janice. She should produce the Star baby if we are successful. That is the purpose for projecting the assisted cone." Janice had confided in her mother Paulina, her wishes to have a love child with James. Paulina recognized and accepted Janice's chosen path. She advised her to seek Djaina's advice. Janice had approached Dljaina with her wishes to have a star child with James. She had assured her that James was more than willing and would perform his part at the appropriate time. I had already approached Dljaina seeking our groups help and purpose for the next use of the CTB. Everyone, but you, was present at our last gathering at Jose's to discuss business. We discussed and planned tonight's cone. Everyone looked forward to tonight's ritual here at the Stone Camp."

"It was decided that today, we are calling the Archangel Gabriella and Father Sky to ask for their help in directing the energies of the planets conjunct with the Moon to Janice. She should conceive the Star baby, if we are successful, at precisely 2:15 when the three planets are conjunct with the moon." Janice had first approached Mary Jane about replacing her in the cone, "so I will have more energy to direct to my personal life. Another understatement to be sure, but Mary Jane had not grasped that the ceremony would be for Janice"

It was only then that Mary Jane noticed that the others had arrived and settled down to meditate and find their inner calm before the ritual Mary Jane immediately went into a light trance as well. None too soon; for but a few minutes passed, when Dljaina the Priestess was saying "We are here to direct the energies of the planets conjunct with the moon to Paulina's daughter Janice. Let us proceed"

They all automatically walked single file past Paulina, to be anointed and cleansed and form a circle In the sanctified area. Once the four corners had been attended, they proceeded to set up a simple cone, rather than the three dimensional star they usually preferred. It had been decided to use the simpler cone; because this was the first time; they worked with the CTB assist. Having not worked with the CTB before; and because of the disastrous results of its misuse, the bi direction of the two cones of the six pointed star seemed too difficult for a first attempt. Dljaina continued "Join hands, and energies to bring up the cone." Mary Jane thought the soft hum of the circular transporter beam in the background sounded like the Au_Ohm, they so often chanted in meditation. She recognized that Paulina had responded with a thought wave to switch on the CTB, just as their energies joined moving around the circle to erect the cone. She could feel their energies mingle as they erected the cone. No, it was more than that. They had become the cone. They were all a whirling cone of Light. Dljaina directed them to call the Archangel Gabriela and sky Father. Their energies were blended with the higher vibrations of the Archangel and Sky Father. It was a feeling of unimaginable bliss Mary Jane was never able to remember what happened between the time the cone touched the Archangel, and the end of the ritual. She returned to full consciousness, as the ritual ended and the cone came down She had a feeling of calm, happiness, knowing the ritual was a success.

She felt she had had an encounter of the fourth kind with the Gods. The others of the cone seemed to share her inner knowing that the ritual was a success. She was the only one, who completely lost consciousness. Most went into a light trance, and remembered everything. Later friends on the outside bribed and cajoled her to tell them, their fortunes. Her mother started asking her advice on all things large and small. She was never the same after the ritual. As soon as the cone was down the ritual participants packed up all candles altar cloths, sacred incense, oils and meditation items. Icon, Everyone, piled into the car pools they came in and headed for Jose's restaurant: except for Major Paulina, who stayed behind to check the video, they had made for the military and to lock up after everyone else had left the Post. They discussed the ritual, as they began to dive into the marvelous restaurant meal, Jose had prepared. All agreed; they had made contact with two beings on a higher plane of vibration. The Archangel Gabriella and sky Father. The military did not recognize Angels They might not even recognize that a connection had been made to a higher plane. Paulina reported that the Archangel and Sky Father were not heard on the video, and because of their intense luminosity they would probably be mistaken as moon beams or other unexplained lights. If by chance, the entities were seen on the video for a brief time when their brilliance dimmed, as they were leaving. The Military observers would have thought they were "space aliens" They were visible in no more than three consecutive frames. Paulina had only detected them by viewing the video, frame by frame. Something she hoped to prevent others from doing. Gabriella and Sky Father helped willingly. They spoke all the earth languages, but found it more convenient to communicate with each other telepathically, as they normally did. They also spoke telepathically to the participants of the cone, so of course, nothing was heard on the tape. Sky Father's large soft glowing green eyes smiled as he spoke to Gabriella. "They called you the Archangel Gabriel when we were here before. How can they have missed the soft femininity that is your being?" He saw her eyes sparkle blue with white flecks, like white water, as he mentally received her reply. "I love your eyes, the color of healing green." Why do you talk so macho when we visit earth?

They are here to learn to communicate in love as we do. Let them witness our bright stars coming together to form a giant sun, in the river of time. Then let them see us separate and go our different ways each a little larger and brighter than before." Sky Father thought about what she said as he replied. "You are right, it is the union of the male and female that make our unique aspects so attractive."

"Men respond to the macho show and it is an irresponsible conceit on my part to provide it."

Gabriella looked at him intently, as his eyes turned coal black with a red fire of passion deep within she heard him continue. "I still remember the feelings of male dominance that held the woman at bay, subservient and separate." It's true, sometimes I feel overwhelmed with earthly passions "was his earnest reply. Gabrielle gazed at James and Janice. Her sparkling eyes now were calm as still blue water. "Look at the two of them" "They are so in love, it permeates his apartment" "Even Paulina feels their love and respects it" Sky Father now turned more serious. "Yes, we will direct the energy to produce the star child. I'm not sure the time is right. I think you and she have much yet to learn about love. They are too young to raise the Star child. Still maybe they do have a chance."

This time it was Gabriella who became defensive. "Love is what matters not age." Sky Father immediately gave way to her wisdom. So it was done and a star child was conceived by Janice, at exactly 2:15 PM James jumped up in what seemed to him only a few short minutes later. He said to Janice, "The old witch is at the door. "Janice quickly dressed, and went to let her mother in. One glance at Janice and Paulina knew the energy had been well received and the star child was conceived. She momentarily thought of calling everyone in the circle to give them the good news. Aloud she said "I dropped by to take you shopping for school clothes." Janice replied, by turning to James, and with a longing look she said, "James, Darling, you remember, I promised Mom to go shopping with her today, at 3 It is 3 now. James kissed Janice goodbye as he mumbled, "wow, the morning really went fast." "Catch you later brat." The old witch could feel his glare. She smiled quietly, and waited patiently. She was thinking, "This house is so quiet and filled with their love. He looks at me like a male dog standing by his bitch, growling and bracing his teeth, ready to fight everyone off for her." "I think he should sense I am not a threat to their love." Janice's cheerful "Come on Mom let's go" broke in on her dark thoughts. Today they called Sky Father and the Archangel Gabriella and they came. The CTB intensified the power of the cone and it was an immediate success. She and Janice would celebrate the success together and she would give thanks to Gabriella and Sky Father by honoring and respecting their radiance as it shone through Janice. She would make sure Janice bought clothes that either, stretched a great deal or were very large to start with. She silently, blessed her daughter, and thanked Sky Father and the Archangel Gabriella.

Edwards Brothers,Inc!
Thorofare, NJ 08086
30 August, 2010
BA2010242